How

the

Rosary

Sister Mary Francis P.C.C.

McCrimmons
Great Wakering, Essex

This Edition published in Great Britain in 1999 by
McCRIMMON PUBLISHING COMPANY LIMITED
10–12 High Street, Great Wakering, Essex SS3 0EQ, England.
Telephone (01702) 218956 Fax (01702) 216082

Email: mccrimmons@dial.pipex.com

First Published in Great Britain in 1975 by
MAYHEW-McCRIMMON LIMITED.

ISBN 0 85597 158 4

Nihil Obstat   Martin Hancock
                                                David Donnelly
Imprimatur   C.D. Creede Vic. Gen.
Brentwood January 30 1975

ACKNOWLEDGMENTS
The scripture texts are taken from the Jerusalem Bible Version of the
Scriptures, copyrighted © in 1966, 1967 and 1968 by Darton, Longman
and Todd Ltd and Doubleday and Co. Inc., and used by permission.

Typeset by McCrimmons in Times 10/10.5pt and Times Italic 12pt
Cover design and layout by Brendan Waller
Cover image by Brendan Waller
Reprographics by Mayhew McCrimmon Printers Ltd, Essex
Printed in Great Britain by Black Bear Press Ltd, Cambridge

Introduction
To the Second Edition

It is a great source of joy to hear how this little book has proved helpful to so many people since its first publication in 1975, and that now a new edition is to be published. The highlight of this is surely the new and inspiring cover design.

Some have found the little book not only a lifeline with regard to distractions, but a stepping stone into deeper understanding of the Gospel message. As they ponder the texts, new lights have been given, and these in turn have helped them to understand other passages more deeply. They have rejoiced in their own experience of the truth that the Word of God is indeed 'living and active'. The new cover somehow portrays this with the small photograph on the front representing the actual scriptural message of the decade we are praying. Then the ongoing enlargement of it in the background conveys our growing and ever deepening understanding of it in prayer through God's grace. (I hope this will not cause the designer to wince!)

The Rosary though, has increasingly become for each one, all that Our Lady longed for us to receive through this devotion. It can also be helpful to select just one key text for each decade and ponder this alone. This can lead on to one text for the whole five decades of each Mystery, such as for the Joyful Mysteries the climax is '...Today in the town of David a saviour has been born to you; he is Christ the Lord. And here is a sign for you: you will find a baby wrapped in swaddling clothes and lying in a manger.' (Luke 2:11-12) In the Sorrowful Mysteries Jesus himself announces the culmination in '...After Jesus had taken the vinegar he said: "It is accomplished"; and bowing his head he gave up his spirit.'(John 19:30) The Glorious Mysteries are each so momentous that one text can be difficult to decide upon, but if one text can bear the fruits of them all would it not be '...And know that I am with you always; yes, to the end of time.' (Matthew 28:20) With us always, and especially so when we listen to him in his Word in praying the Rosary.

Can I now conclude this second introduction by sharing an incident reported to me. A friend, away from home, went to the local Parish Church for Mass. The Congregation was unknown to her. As she knelt down, she noticed on the bench just in front of her, the remains of a very much used copy of *How to Pray the Rosary*. At the end of Mass, as the lady turned to collect her little book and beads, my friend could not resist it, and told the lady that she knew the author, and knew she would be so pleased to hear how much used her little book had obviously been. To her joy, the lady's face seemed to light up, and she exclaimed. 'Oh please will you tell her how grateful I am, for it has been such a help...'.

How grateful I am too for this kind message, and for the many heartwarming letters and cards sent so kindly by those using this little book. How precious to the Mother of God must be such dear souls. May our Mother and Queen of the most holy Rosary pray for us all, and help us to meditate ever anew on these Mysteries in her Holy Rosary that, as we pray in the concluding prayer, '…we may both follow the example that they give and obtain the salvation that they promise…' through her dear Son and our loving Saviour, Jesus Christ, Amen.

Sr. Mary Francis.

Sister Mary Francis, P.C.C.

Poor Clare Monastery
Bulwell
Nottingham

May 1999

Sister Mary Francis was born and educated in London. In 1953 she entered the Monastery where she is now Abbess.

Through the years, in her counselling and wide correspondence, she has come in contact with many who have voiced their difficulties in prayer, especially with regard to the rosary. It was in response to their deeply felt need that this book was written.

Introduction

'Sister, I have packed up trying to say the rosary. It was just a waste of time for me. Rattling off all those 'Hail Marys' seemed so pointless. I know you are supposed to think about the mysteries, but my thoughts on them don't stretch very far...'

This is just one voice, but many thousands of people have abandoned, or are gradually abandoning, the praying of the rosary. The reasons are numerous, but many, it seems, find they are just 'saying it' and not 'praying it', and the ensuing feeling of the 'waste of time' and 'pointlessness' of it, are major factors in their deciding that it is something more suited to the mentality of people of former ages.

Meanwhile, many are finding that the reading and study of Scripture is much more helpful and relevant to our needs of today, both spiritually and intellectually. Yet, to see the study of Scripture, and the praying of the rosary, as two separate. if not opposing, entities, is surely to reveal that one of the purposes of the rosary has been forgotten: for what is the rosary if not a series of prayerful reflections on that kernel of Scripture which most concerns us, namely the Good News of our Salvation?

Leaving this aspect for the moment, another difficulty some have in trying to pray the rosary, is that they cannot keep their mind on the mysteries. They begin with often just a momentary and hazy thought on the subject of the mystery, and recite the 'Our Father' and 'Hail Marys', and within no time their thoughts are away on a thousand and one distractions, during which the decade passes, and sometimes other decades, or even the entire rosary, without any return of thought to the subject of their prayer. By the end of such rosaries, there is more a feeling of frustration, depression or guilt, instead of all the help and inspiration and encouragement Our Lady meant to be derived from it.

The trouble then, seems to stem from the beginning, from that 'momentary, hazy thought' of the mystery. If we could, therefore, try to remove the 'haze', we should at least make a good beginning, and what could be better for this purpose than a short, prayerful reading of the subject of the mystery in the Bible? However, if our mind is very preoccupied with the cares of our daily life, it may need further help, to keep it from wandering. In this case, instead of reading at once all the passage about the mystery in the Bible, it may be found more helpful if it was divided into parts, and then to prayerfully reflect on one part at a time while reciting each 'Hail Mary' of the decade.

There are many times and places when and where we can pray the rosary, but it would not be possible to carry around a Bible with us, and so, for convenience, I have collected a group of quotations for each mystery which may be found helpful. There are so many others which may be preferred, that each person would be advised to compile their own 'Bible Rosary', or make their own alterations or additions to this one. Where possible, I have taken the actual Gospel narratives, but in others, especially for the Assumption and Crowning of Our Lady, I have drawn from those Scriptural texts allocated to the feasts in the Missal and Breviary.

Some may object that this method may be alright in the beginning, but that the repeated reading of the same texts would lead to a deadening of their impact. I think in this we do, to a certain extent, get what we expect from God. If we do not expect much – well then, just so, it is we who restrict him; but the more we expect and hope, the more it seems we allow him entrance to give help and light and understanding. We must remember too, that the Word of God is 'living and active'.

Perhaps we can liken such readings of Scripture to the workings of a cigarette lighter. The 'Word of God', is represented by the large flint, we the small one. Our reading of the Word is the bringing of the small flint into contact with the large one. Then, what we have read and listened to in our heart, gradually forms the wick that enters and is absorbed by the petrol of the Holy Spirit. While reading thus, it happens that a special contact is made, a light or spark from the flint ignites the wick of our reading, and it is suddenly illumined, and the passage has a new or deeper meaning for us.

We too, in this way, share a little in the experience of the disciples on their way to Emmaus. Our eyes too are opened, and we recognise him, and our hearts burn within us as he talks to us on our way. It is encouraging for us that the disciples seem to be marvelling when they said to each other, 'Did not our hearts burn within us as he talked to us on the road and explained the scriptures to us?' (Luke 24:32), for had they not been listening to the Word continually during Our Lord's public ministry? There had been much 'wick preparing' for them too then, and then came their ignition and recognition.

In our busy world today, time – and opportunity – is another problem for many with regard to the rosary, and this form of Bible Rosary will take a little longer. If extra time is not possible, would it not be better, to begin with, to pray fewer decades each day, if this will mean so much more to us than just saying hastily five or more decades? Gradually, as repeated readings of the Scripture texts enter our minds and hearts, there may not be the same need to pray the rosary in this way, for we shall have a new possessing of the 'Good News' within us.

It may be found helpful though, from time to time to return to this form of praying the rosary, especially in times of stress and anxiety, when our minds are preoccupied with worries. At such times, to be able to leave our troubles in God's keeping for a while, and enter in prayer to reflecting on the 'Good News', and all it entailed for Christ for us, has a strengthening consolation all its own.

Each decade or mystery has a special message, but every one reveals to us more deeply God's love for us, his sending of his only-begotten Son down to earth for love of us, his Passion and death for love of us, and then in the Glorious Mysteries, we ponder on the consummation of it all; the end which is the beginning, and in which, in the Mystical Body we are each incorporated.

As we pray the rosary, the role of Our Lady in our salvation will also come to have an ever deepening meaning for us; from her first humble acceptance in the Annunciation, to become the Mother of God, to her acceptance on Calvary to be the Mother of all men, the brethren of her Divine Son. With Jesus, Mary too, is with us always.

Finally in the third Eucharistic Prayer of the Mass, we pray, 'Strengthen in faith and love your pilgrim Church...' Was it not for this purpose that Our Lady introduced to Saint Dominic the devotion or prayer which we call the rosary?

In the early Church, with its Jewish background, there would have been the strong oral tradition in the teaching of the Faith. The subjects of the mysteries of the rosary would have been recounted constantly, and pondered on, for there was no written form of the Gospels. Then as the centuries passed, the Church grew and developed in the cultural developments of the civilisations of her members.

Printing was one development, and the Word of God in Scripture, was gradually made available to more and more people. One wonders though, if, having removed much of the need of the former oral tradition, whether the printed form having become 'taken for granted' was less and less read and pondered on by the members of the Church, and a haze began to form in the minds of many.

The wheat of the Good News was not without its cockle, and heresies were cropping up, and so it was Our Lady came with the rosary, so relevant to the needs of the people of Saint Dominic's time. Is it any less relevant to our needs today, when the faith and love of the Pilgrim Church are so much in need of strengthening? It is to our loss then, that although in the rosary there is a tremendous source of grace to strengthen us in our faith and love, so many are in fact rejecting it. Would that those who have 'packed up trying', would unpack their efforts and try again this way.

May I conclude then with the quotation with which I have concluded the last mystery of the rosary:

> 'Let us be confident then in approaching the throne of grace, that we shall have mercy from him and find grace when we are in need of help.'   (*Hebrews 4:16*)

Sister Mary Francis P.C.C.

Feast of the Solemnity of
Mary the Mother of God.

The Prayers
of the Rosary

The prayers used in the rosary, for those not familiar with them, are:-

Our Father who are in heaven, hallowed be thy name. Thy kingdom come. Thy will be done on earth as it is in heaven. Give us this day our daily bread, and forgive us our trespasses, as we forgive those who trespass against us. And lead us not into temptation, but deliver us from evil. Amen.

Hail Mary, full of grace, the Lord is with thee. Blessed art thou among women, and blessed is the fruit of thy womb, Jesus. Holy Mary, Mother of God, pray for us sinners, now, and at the hour of our death. Amen.

Glory be to the Father, and to the Son, and to the Holy Spirit. As it was in the beginning, is now, and ever shall be, world without end. Amen.

The Joyful Mysteries

The Annunciation

Our Father.

1. In the sixth month the angel Gabriel was sent by God to a town in Galilee called Nazareth, to a virgin betrothed to a man named Joseph, of the House of David; and the virgin's name was Mary. *Luke 1:26-27*
Hail Mary.

2. He went in and said to her: 'Rejoice, so highly favoured! The Lord is with you. *Luke 1:28*
Hail Mary.

3. She was deeply disturbed by these words and asked herself what this greeting could mean. *Luke 1:29*
Hail Mary.

4. But the angel said to her: 'Mary, do not be afraid; you have won God's favour. *Luke 1:30*
Hail Mary.

5. 'Listen! You are to conceive and bear a son, and you must name him Jesus. He will be great and will be

called Son of the Most High. The Lord God will give him the throne of his ancestor David; he will rule over the House of Jacob for ever and his reign will have no end. *Luke 1:31-33*

Hail Mary.

6. Mary said to the angel: 'But how can this come about, since I am a virgin?' *Luke 1:34*

Hail Mary.

7. 'The Holy Spirit will come upon you,' the angel answered, 'and the power of the Most High will cover you with its shadow. And so the child will be holy and will be called Son of God. *Luke 1:35*

Hail Mary.

8. 'Know this too: your kinswoman Elizabeth has, in her old age, herself conceived a son, and she whom people called barren is now in her sixth month, for nothing is impossible to God.' *Luke 1:36-37*

Hail Mary.

9. 'I am the handmaid of the Lord,' said Mary, 'let what you have said be done to me.' *Luke 1:38*

Hail Mary.

10. And the angel left her. *Luke 1:38*

Hail Mary.

Glory be to the Father, and to the Son, and to the Holy Spirit; as it was in the beginning, is now, and ever shall be, world without end. Amen.

The Visitation

Our Father

1. Mary set out at that time and went as quickly as she could to a town in the hill country of Judah. She went into Zechariah's house and greeted Elizabeth.

   Luke 1:39-40
   Hail Mary.

2. Now as soon as Elizabeth heard Mary's greeting the child leapt in her womb and Elizabeth was filled with the Holy Spirit. *Luke 1:41*
   Hail Mary.

3. She gave a loud cry and said: 'Of all women you are the most blessed, and blessed is the fruit of your womb. *Luke 1:42*
   Hail Mary.

4. 'Why should I be honoured with a visit from the mother of my Lord? For the moment your greeting reached my ears, the child in my womb leapt for joy. Yes, blessed is she who believed that the promise made her by the Lord would be fulfilled.' *Luke 1:43-45*
   Hail Mary.

5. And Mary said:
   'My soul proclaims the greatness of the Lord and my spirit exults in God my saviour; because he has looked upon his lowly handmaid.

   Luke 1:46-47
   Hail Mary.

6. 'Yes from this day forward all
generations will call me blessed,
for the Almighty has done great things for me.

Luke 1:48
Hail Mary.

7. 'Holy is his name,
and his mercy reaches from age to age
for those who fear him. *Luke 1:49-50*
Hail Mary.

8. 'He has shown the power of his arm,
He has routed the proud of heart.
He has pulled down princes from their thrones
and exalted the lowly.
The hungry he has filled with good things,
the rich sent empty away. *Luke 1:51-53*
Hail Mary.

9. 'He has come to the help of Israel his servant,
mindful of his mercy – according to the promise he
made to our ancestors – of his mercy to Abraham and
to his descendants for ever.' *Luke 1:54-55*
Hail Mary.

10. Mary stayed with Elizabeth about three months and
then went back home. *Luke 1:56*
Hail Mary.

Glory be to the Father.

The Nativity

Our Father

1. Now at this time Caesar Augustus issued a decree for a census of the whole world to be taken. So Joseph set out from the town of Nazareth in Galilee and travelled up to Judea, to the town of David called Bethlehem, since he was of David's House and line, in order to be registered together with Mary, his betrothed, who was with child. *Luke 2:1,4-5*

   Hail Mary.

2. While they were there the time came for her to have her child, and she gave birth to a son, her first born. *Luke 2:6-7*

   Hail Mary.

3. She wrapped him in swaddling clothes, and laid him in a manger because there was no room for them at the inn. *Luke 2:7*

   Hail Mary.

4. In the countryside close by there were shepherds who lived in the fields and took it in turns to watch their flocks during the night. The angel of the Lord appeared to them and the glory of the Lord shone round them. They were terrified, but the angel said: 'Do not be afraid. Listen, I bring you news of great joy, a joy to be shared by the whole people. *Luke 2:8-10*

   Hail Mary.

5. 'Today in the town of David a saviour has been born

to you; he is Christ the Lord. And here is a sign for you: you will find a baby wrapped in swaddling clothes and lying in a manger.' *Luke 2:11-12*

Hail Mary.

6. And suddenly with the angel there was a great throng of the heavenly host, praising God and singing: 'Glory to God in the highest heaven, and peace to men who enjoy his favour.'*Luke 2:13-14*

Hail Mary.

7. Now when the angels had gone from them into heaven, the shepherds said to one another: 'Let us go to Bethlehem and see this thing that has happened which the Lord has made known to us.' *Luke 2:15*

Hail Mary.

8. So they hurried away and found Mary and Joseph, and the baby lying in the manger. When they saw the child they repeated what they had been told about him, and everyone who heard it was astonished at what the shepherds had to say. *Luke 2:16-18*

Hail Mary.

9. As for Mary, she treasured all these things and pondered them in her heart. *Luke 2:19*

Hail Mary.

10. And the shepherds went back glorifying and praising God for all they had heard and seen; it was exactly as they had been told. *Luke 2:20*

Hail Mary. **Glory be to the Father.**

The Presentation

Our Father

1. And when the day came for them to be purified as laid
    down by the Law of Moses, they took him up to
    Jerusalem to present him to the Lord   *Luke 2:22*
                                                   Hail Mary.

2. – observing what stands written in the Law of the Lord:
    Every first-born male must be consecrated to the
    Lord –   *Luke 2:23*
                                                   Hail Mary.

3. and also offer in sacrifice, in accordance with what is
    said in the Law of the Lord, a pair of turtledoves or two
    young pigeons.   *Luke 2:24*
                                                   Hail Mary.

4. Now in Jerusalem there was a man named Simeon. He
    was an upright and devout man; he looked forward to
    Israel's comforting and the Holy Spirit rested on him. It
    had been revealed to him by the Holy Spirit that he
    would not see death until he had set eyes on the Christ
    of the Lord.   *Luke 2:25-26*
                                                   Hail Mary.

5. Prompted by the Spirit he came to the Temple; and
    when the parents brought in the child Jesus to do for
    him what the Law required, he took him into his arms
    and blessed God;   *Luke 2:27-28*
                                                   Hail Mary.

6. and he said:
    'Now, Master, you can let your servant go in peace,
    just as you promised;
    because my eyes have seen the salvation which you
    have prepared for all the nations to see,
    a light to enlighten the pagans
    and the glory of your people Israel.'   *Luke 2:28-32*
                                              Hail Mary.

7. As the child's father and mother stood there wondering
    at the things that were being said about him, Simeon
    blessed them   *Luke 2:33-34*
                                              Hail Mary.

8. and said to Mary his mother: 'You see this child; he is
    destined for the fall and for the rising of many in Israel,
    destined to be a sign that is rejected – and a sword will
    pierce your own soul too – so that the secret thoughts of
    many may be laid bare.'   *Luke 2:34-35*
                                              Hail Mary.

9. There was a prophetess also, Anna the daughter of
    Phanuel, of the tribe of Asher. She was well on in years.
    Her days of girlhood over, she had been married for
    seven years before becoming a widow. She was now
    eighty-four years old and never left the Temple, serving
    God night and day with fasting and prayer. She came by
    just at that moment and began to praise God; and she
    spoke of the child to all who looked forward to the
    deliverance of Jerusalem.   *Luke 2:36-38*
                                              Hail Mary.

10. When they had done everything the Law of the Lord
    required, they went back to Galilee. to their own town
    of Nazareth. *Luke 2:39*
    Hail Mary.

Glory be to the Father.

The Finding in the Temple

Our Father

1. Meanwhile the child grew to maturity, and he was
    filled with wisdom; and God's favour was with him.
    Luke 2:40
    Hail Mary.

2. Every year his parents used to go to Jerusalem for the
    feast of the Passover. When he was twelve years old,
    they went up for the feast as usual. *Luke 2:41-42*
    Hail Mary.

3. When they were on their way home after the feast, the
    boy Jesus stayed behind in Jerusalem without his
    parents knowing it. *Luke 2:43*
    Hail Mary.

4. They assumed he was with the caravan, and it was only
    after a day's journey that they went to look for him
    among their relations and acquaintances. When they
    failed to find him they went back to Jerusalem looking
    for him everywhere. *Luke 2:44-45*
    Hail Mary.

5. Three days later, they found him in the Temple, sitting among the doctors, listening to them, and asking them questions; and all those who heard him were astounded at his intelligence and his replies.   *Luke 2:46-47*

    Hail Mary.

6. They were overcome when they saw him, and his mother said to him: 'My child, why have you done this to us? See how worried your father and I have been, looking for you.'   *Luke 2:48*

    Hail Mary.

7. 'Why were you looking for me?' he replied. 'Did you not know that I must be busy with my Father's affairs?'   *Luke 2:49*

    Hail Mary.

8. But they did not understand what he meant. *Luke 2:50*

    Hail Mary.

9. He then went down with them and came to Nazareth and lived under their authority.   *Luke 2:51*

    Hail Mary.

10. His mother stored up all these things in her heart. And Jesus increased in wisdom, in stature, and in favour with God and men.   *Luke 2:52*

    Hail Mary.

Glory be to the Father.

The Sorrowful Mysteries

The Agony in the Garden

Our Father

1. Then Jesus came with them to a small estate called
   Gethsemane; and he said to his disciples: 'Stay here
   while I go over there to pray.'   *Matthew 26:36*
                                                  Hail Mary.

2. He took Peter and the two sons of Zebedee with him.
   And sadness came over him, and great distress.
                                                  Matthew 26:37
                                                  Hail Mary.

3. Then he said to them: 'My soul is sorrowful to the
   point of death. Wait here and keep awake with me.'
                                                  Matthew 26:38
                                                  Hail Mary.

4. And going on a little further he fell on his face and
   prayed. 'My Father,' he said, 'if it is possible, let this
   cup pass me by. Nevertheless, let it be as you, not I,
   would have it.'   *Matthew 26:39*
                                                  Hail Mary.

5. He came back to the disciples and found them sleeping,
    and he said to Peter: 'So you had not the strength to
    keep awake with me one hour? You should be awake,
    and praying not to be put to the test. The spirit is
    willing, but the flesh is weak.'   *Matthew 26:40-41*
                                                  Hail Mary.

6. Again a second time, he went away and prayed: 'My
    Father,' he said, 'if this cup cannot pass by without my
    drinking it, your will be done!'   *Matthew 26:42*
                                                  Hail Mary.

7. Then an angel appeared to him, coming from heaven to
    give him strength.   *Luke 22:43*
                                                  Hail Mary.

8. In his anguish he prayed even more earnestly, and his
    sweat fell to the ground like great drops of blood.
                                                  Luke 22:44
                                                  Hail Mary.

9. When he rose from prayer he went to the disciples and
    found them sleeping for sheer grief.   *Luke 22:45*
    'You can sleep on now and take your rest. Now the hour
    has come when the Son of Man is to be betrayed into
    the hands of sinners.   *Matthew 26:45*
                                                  Hail Mary.

10. 'Get up! Let us go! My betrayer is already close at
    hand.' He was still speaking when Judas, one of the
    Twelve, appeared, and with him a large number of men

armed with swords and clubs, sent by the chief priests
and elders of the people.   *Matthew 26:46-47*

Hail Mary.

Glory be to the Father.

The Scourging of Jesus at the Pillar

Our Father

1. So Pilate, anxious to placate the crowd, released
    Barabbas for them and, having ordered Jesus to be
    scourged, handed him over to be crucified. *Mark 15:15*

    Hail Mary.

2, Now all this happened to fulfil the prophecies in
    scripture. Then all the disciples deserted him and ran
    away.   *Matthew 26:56*

    Hail Mary.

3. Meanwhile the men who guarded Jesus were mocking
    and beating him.   *Luke 22:63*

    Hail Mary.

4. And yet ours were the sufferings he bore,
    ours the sorrows he carried.
    But we, we thought of him as someone punished,
    struck by God, and brought low.
    Yet he was pierced through for our faults,
    crushed for our sins.   *Isaiah 53:4-5*

    Hail Mary.

5.   For my part, I made no resistance,
     neither did I turn away.
     I offered my back to those who struck me,
     my cheeks to those who tore at my beard;
     I did not cover my face
     against insult and spittle.   *Isaiah 50:5-6*
                                            Hail Mary.

6.   ...from the sole of the foot to the head
     there is not a sound spot:
     wounds, bruises, open sores
     not dressed, not bandaged,
     not soothed with oil.   *Isaiah 1:6*
                                            Hail Mary.

7.   Ploughmen have ploughed on my back longer and
     longer furrows,   *Psalm 129:3*
                                            Hail Mary.

8.   I have trodden the winepress alone.
     Of the men of my people not one was with me.
                                            Isaiah 63:3
                                            Hail Mary.

9.   I will punish their sins with the rod
     and their crimes with the whip,   *Psalm 89:32*
                                            Hail Mary.

10. On him lies a punishment that brings us peace, and
     through his wounds we are healed.   *Isaiah 53:5*
                                            Hail Mary.

Glory be to the Father.

The Crowning of Jesus with Thorns

Our Father.

1. The soldiers led him away to the inner part of the
    palace, that is, the Praetorium, and called the whole
    cohort together.   *Mark 15:16*
                                                        Hail Mary.

2. ...and after this, the soldiers twisted some thorns into
    a crown and put it on his head, and dressed him in a
    purple robe.   *John 19:2*
                                                        Hail Mary.

3. They kept coming up to him and saying:
    'Hail, king of the Jews!' and they slapped him
    in the face.   *John 19:3*
                                                        Hail Mary.

4. If the virtuous man is God's son, God will
    take his part
    and rescue him from the clutches of his enemies.
    Let us test him with cruelty and with torture,
    and thus explore this gentleness of his
    and put his endurance to the proof.   *Wisdom 2:18-19*
                                                        Hail Mary.

5. They struck his head with a reed and spat on him;
    and they went down on their knees to do him homage.
                                                        Mark 15:19
                                                        Hail Mary.

6. Jesus then came out wearing the crown of thorns and the purple robe. Pilate said: 'Here is the man.'

    John 19:5
    Hail Mary.

7. As the crowds were appalled on seeing him
    – so disfigured did he look
    that he seemed no longer human –
    so will the crowds be astonished at him,
    and kings stand speechless before him;
    for they shall see something never told
    and witness something never heard before:

    Isaiah 52:14-15
    Hail Mary.

8. And when they had finished making fun of him, they took off the cloak and dressed him in his own clothes.

    Matthew 27:31
    Hail Mary.

9. Let us condemn him to a shameful death
    since he will be looked after – we have his word for it.

    Wisdom 2:20
    Hail Mary.

10. So in the end Pilate handed him over to them to be crucified.

    John 19:16
    Hail Mary.

Glory be to the Father.

Jesus Carries His Cross

Our Father.

1. They led him out to crucify him. *Mark 15:21*
    Hail Mary.

2. As they were leading him away they seized on a man,
    Simon from Cyrene, who was coming in from the
    country, and made him shoulder the cross and carry it
    behind Jesus. *Luke 23:26*
    Hail Mary.

3. Large numbers of people followed him, and of women
    too, who mourned and lamented for him. *Luke 23:27*
    Hail Mary.

4. But Jesus turned to them and said:
    'Daughters of Jerusalem, do not weep for me;
    Luke 23:28
    Hail Mary.

5. '…weep rather for yourselves and for your children.
    Luke 23:28
    Hail Mary.

6. 'For the days will surely come when people will say:
    "Happy are those who are barren, the wombs that
    have never borne, the breasts that have never
    suckled!" Then they will begin to say to the
    mountains: "Fall on us!", to the hills, "Cover us!" For

if men use the green wood like this, what will happen
when it is dry?'   *Luke 23:29-31*
                                              Hail Mary.

7. We had all gone astray like sheep,
    each taking his own way,
    and Yahweh burdened him
    with the sins of all of us.   *Isaiah 53:7*
                                              Hail Mary.

8. Harshly dealt with, he bore it humbly,
    he never opened his mouth,
    like a lamb that is led to the slaughter-house,
    like a sheep that is dumb before its shearers
    never opening its mouth.   *Isaiah 53:6*
                                              Hail Mary.

9. Now with him they were also leading out two other
    criminals to be executed.   *Luke 23:32*
                                              Hail Mary.

10. They brought Jesus to the place called Golgotha,
    which means the place of the skull.   *Mark 15:22*
                                              Hail Mary.

Glory be to the Father.

The Crucifixion

Our Father.

1. When they had reached a place called Golgotha, that
    is, the place of the skull, they gave him wine to drink
    mixed with gall, which he tasted but refused to drink.

    Matthew 27:33-34

    Hail Mary.

2. It was the third hour when they crucified him.

    Mark 15:25

    When they had finished crucifying him they shared
    out his clothing by casting lots, and then sat down and
    stayed there keeping guard over him.

    Matthew 27:35-36

    Hail Mary.

3. Above his head was placed the charge against him; it
    read: 'This is Jesus, the King of the Jews.' At the same
    time two robbers were crucified with him, one on the
    right and one on the left. *Matthew 27:37-38*

    Hail Mary.

4. The passers-by jeered at him: *Matthew 27:39*
    One of the criminals hanging there abused him. 'Are
    you not the Christ?' he said. 'Save yourself and us as
    well.' But the other spoke up and rebuked him. 'Have
    you no fear of God at all?' he said. 'You got the same
    sentence as he did, but in our case we deserved it: we
    are paying for what we did. But this man has done
    nothing wrong. Jesus', he said, 'remember me when

you come into your Kingdom.' 'Indeed, I promise
you,' he replied, 'today you will be with me in
paradise.'   *Luke 23:39-43*
                                                    Hail Mary.

5.   Near the cross of Jesus stood his mother and his
     mother's sister, Mary the wife of Clopas, and Mary of
     Magdala. Seeing his mother and the disciple he loved
     standing near her, Jesus said to his mother: 'Woman,
     this is your son.' Then to the disciple he said: 'This is
     your mother'. And from that moment the disciple
     made a place for her in his home.   *John 19:25-27*
                                                    Hail Mary.

6.   It was now about the sixth hour and, with the sun
     eclipsed, a darkness came over the whole land until
     the ninth hour. The veil of the Temple was torn right
     down the middle.   *Luke 23:44-45*
                                                    Hail Mary.

7.   And about the ninth hour, Jesus cried out in a loud
     voice: 'Eli, Eli, lama sabachthani?' that is: 'My God,
     my God, why have you deserted me?'   *Matthew 27:46*
                                                    Hail Mary.

8.   After this, Jesus knew that everything had now been
     completed, and to fulfil the scripture perfectly he said:
     'I am thirsty.'
     A jar full of vinegar stood there, so putting a sponge

soaked in the vinegar on a hyssop stick they held it up
to his mouth.   *John 19:28-29*

                                                      Hail Mary.

9.   After Jesus had taken the vinegar he said: 'It is
accomplished;' and bowing his head he gave up his
spirit.   *John 19:30*

                                                      Hail Mary.

10. When the centurion saw what had taken place, he
gave praise to God and said: 'This was a great and
good man.' And when all the people who had gathered
for the spectacle saw what had happened, they went
home beating their breasts.   *Luke 23:47-48*

                                                      Hail Mary.

Glory be to the Father.

The Glorious Mysteries

The Resurrection

Our Father.

1. When the Sabbath was over, Mary of Magdala, Mary
    the mother of James, and Salome, bought spices with
    which to go and anoint him. And very early in the
    morning on the first day of the week they went to the
    tomb, just as the sun was rising.   *Mark 16:1-2*
                                              Hail Mary.

2. And all at once there was a violent earthquake, for the
    angel of the Lord, descending from heaven, came and
    rolled away the stone and sat on it. His face was like
    lightning, his robe white as snow. The guards were so
    shaken, so frightened of him, that they were like dead
    men.   *Matthew 28:2-4*
                                              Hail Mary.

3. But the angel spoke; and he said to the women: 'There
    is no need for you to be afraid. I know you are
    looking for Jesus, who was crucified. He is not here,
    for he has risen, as he said he would. Come and see

the place where he lay, then go quickly and tell his disciples: "He has risen from the dead and now he is going before you to Galilee; it is there you will see him." Now I have told you.'   *Matthew 28:5-7*

Hail Mary.

4. Filled with awe and great joy the women came quickly away from the tomb and ran to tell the disciples. And there, coming to meet them, was Jesus. 'Greetings,' he said. And the women came up to him and, falling down before him, clasped his feet.

    Matthew 28:8-9

Hail Mary.

5. Then Jesus said to them: 'Do not be afraid; go and tell my brothers that they must leave for Galilee; they will see me there.'   *Matthew 28:10*

Hail Mary.

6. In the evening of that same day, the first day of the week, the doors were closed in the room where the disciples were, for fear of the Jews. Jesus came and stood among them. He said to them: 'Peace be with you.'   *John 20:19*

Hail Mary.

7. In a state of alarm and fright, they thought they were seeing a ghost. But he said: 'Why are you so agitated, and why are these doubts rising in your hearts? Look at my hands and feet; yes, it is I indeed. Touch me and

see for yourselves; a ghost has no flesh and bones as you can see I have.' *Luke 24:37-39*
Hail Mary.

8. And as he said this he showed them his hands and feet. Their joy was so great that they still could not believe it, and they stood there dumbfounded; so he said to them: 'Have you anything here to eat?' And they offered him a piece of grilled fish, which he took and ate before their eyes. *Luke 24:40-43*
Hail Mary.

9. Then he told them: 'This is what I meant when I said, while I was still with you, that everything written about me in the Law of Moses, in the Prophets and in the Psalms, has to be fulfilled.' He then opened their minds to understand the scriptures, *Luke 24:44-45*
Hail Mary.

10. and he said to them: 'So you see how it is written that the Christ would suffer and on the third day rise from the dead, and that, in his name, repentance for the forgiveness of sins would be preached to all the nations, beginning from Jerusalem. You are witnesses to this.' *Luke 24:46-48*
Hail Mary.

Glory be to the Father.

The Ascension

Our Father.

1. He had shown himself alive to them after his Passion
   by many demonstrations: for forty days he had
   continued to appear to them and tell them about the
   kingdom of God. *Acts 1:3*
   Hail Mary.

2. ...the eleven disciples set out for Galilee, to the
   mountain where Jesus had arranged to meet them.
   When they saw him they fell down before him, though
   some hesitated. *Matthew 28:16-17*
   Hail Mary.

3. Jesus came up and spoke to them. He said: 'All
   authority in heaven and on earth has been given to me.
   Matthew 28:18
   Hail Mary.

4. 'Go, therefore, make disciples of all the nations;
   baptize them in the name of the Father and of the Son
   and of the Holy Spirit, *Matthew 28:19*
   Hail Mary.

5. 'and teach them to observe all the commands I gave
   you. And know that I am with you always; yes, to the
   end of time.' *Matthew 28:20*
   Hail Mary.

6. As he said this he was lifted up while they looked on, and a cloud took him from their sight. *Acts 1:9*
Hail Mary.

7. And so the Lord Jesus, after he had spoken to them, was taken up into heaven: there at the right hand of God he took his place, *Mark 16:19*
Hail Mary.

8. They were still staring into the sky when suddenly two men in white were standing near them. *Acts 1:10*
Hail Mary.

9. …and they said: 'Why are you men from Galilee standing here looking into the sky? Jesus who has been taken up from you into heaven, this same Jesus will come back in the same way as you have seen him go there.' *Acts 1:11*
Hail Mary.

10. So from the Mount of Olives, as it is called, they went back to Jerusalem. a short distance away, no more than a Sabbath walk; *Acts 1:12*
Hail Mary.

Glory be to the Father

The Descent of the Holy Spirit

Our Father.

1. 'And now I am sending down to you what the Father has promised. Stay in the city then, until you are clothed with power from on high.'   *Luke 24:49*
                                                                                                       Hail Mary.

2. …and when they reached the city they went to the upper room where they were staying; …All these (the eleven apostles) joined in continuous prayer, together with several women, including Mary the mother of Jesus, and with his brothers.   *Acts 1:13-14*
                                                                                                       Hail Mary.

3. When Pentecost day came round, they had all met in one room, when suddenly they heard what sounded like a powerful wind from heaven, the noise of which filled the entire house in which they were sitting; and something appeared to them that seemed like tongues of fire; these separated and came to rest on the head of each of them.   *Acts 2:1-3*
                                                                                                       Hail Mary.

4. They were all filled with the Holy Spirit, and began to speak foreign languages as the Spirit gave them the gift of speech.
   Now there were devout men living in Jerusalem from every nation under heaven, and at this sound they all

assembled, each one bewildered to hear these men
speaking his own language. *Acts 2:4-6*
Hail Mary.

5. Everyone was amazed and unable to explain it; they
    asked one another what it all meant. Some, however,
    laughed it off. 'They have been drinking too much
    new wine,' they said. *Acts 2:12-13*
    Hail Mary.

6. Then Peter stood up with the Eleven and addressed
    them in a loud voice:
    '…this is what the prophet spoke of:
    In the days to come – it is the Lord who speaks –
    I will pour out my spirit on all mankind.
    Their sons and daughters shall prophesy,
    your young men shall see visions,
    your old men shall dream dreams.
    Even on my slaves, men and women,
    in those days, I will pour out my spirit…'
    Acts 2:14, 16-18
    Hail Mary.

7. God raised this man Jesus to life, and all of us are
    witnesses to that. Now raised to the heights by God's
    right hand, he has received from the Father the Holy
    Spirit, who was promised, and what you see and hear
    is the outpouring of that Spirit. *Acts 2:32-33*
    Hail Mary.

8. ...the whole House of Israel can be certain that God
has made this Jesus whom you crucified both Lord
and Christ.
Hearing this, they were cut to the heart and said to
Peter and the apostles: 'What must we do, brothers?'
'You must repent,' Peter answered, 'and every one of
you must be baptised in the name of Jesus Christ for
the forgiveness of your sins, and you will receive the
gift of the Holy Spirit.   *Acts 2:36-38*
Hail Mary.

9. 'The promise that was made is for you and your
children, and for all those who are far away, for all
those whom the Lord our God will call to himself.'
Acts 2:39
Hail Mary.

10. He spoke to them for a long time using many
arguments, and he urged them: 'Save yourselves from
this perverse generation.' They were convinced by his
arguments, and they accepted what he said and were
baptised. That very day about three thousand were
added to their number.   *Acts 2:40-41*
Hail Mary.

Glory be to the Father.

The Assumption of Our Lady

Our Father.

1. But Christ has in fact been raised from the dead, the
    first-fruits of all who have fallen asleep…
    Just as all men die in Adam, so all men will be
    brought to life in Christ; but all of them in their proper
    order: Christ as the first-fruits and then, after the
    coming of Christ, those who belong to him.

    1 Corinthians 15:20, 22-23

    Hail Mary.

2. When this perishable nature has put on
    imperishability, and when this mortal nature has put
    on immortality, then the words of the scripture will
    come true: Death is swallowed up in victory. Death,
    where is your victory? Death, where is your sting?
    Now the sting of death is sin, and sin gets its power
    from the Law. So let us thank God for giving us the
    victory through our Lord Jesus Christ.

    1 Corinthians 15:54-57

    Hail Mary.

3. …the ones he chose specially long ago and intended
    to become true images of his Son, so that his Son
    might be the eldest of many brothers. He called those
    he intended for this; those he called justified, and with
    those he justified he shared his glory. *Romans 8:29-30*

    Hail Mary.

4. For we know that when the tent that we live in on
    earth is folded up, there is a house built by God for us,
    an everlasting home not made by human hands, in the
    heavens.   *2 Corinthians 5:1*
                                               Hail Mary.

5. Now a great sign appeared in heaven: a woman,
    adorned with the sun, standing on the moon, and with
    the twelve stars on her head for a crown.
                                               Revelation 12:1
                                               Hail Mary.

6. May you be blessed, my daughter,
    by God Most High,
    beyond all women on earth;
    and may the Lord God be blessed,
    the Creator of heaven and earth,
    by whose guidance you cut off the head
    of the leader of our enemies.   *Judith 13:23-24*
                                               Hail Mary.

7. The trust you have shown
    shall not pass from the memories of men,
    but shall ever remind them of the power of God.
    God grant you to be always held in honour,
    and rewarded with blessings,   *Judith 13:25*
                                               Hail Mary.

8. You are the glory of Jerusalem!
    You are the great pride of Israel!
    You are the highest honour of our race!

May you be blessed by the Lord Almighty
in all the days to come! *Judith 15:10*
Hail Mary.

9. Who is this arising like the dawn,
fair as the moon,
resplendent as the sun,
terrible as an army with banners?
Who is this coming up from the desert
leaning on her Beloved? *Song of Songs 6:9, 8:5*
Hail Mary.

10. For Yahweh has chosen Zion,
desiring this to be his home:
Here I will stay for ever,
this is the home I have chosen. *Psalm 132:13-14*
Hail Mary.

Glory be to the Father.

The Crowning of Our Lady in Heaven

Our Father.

1.   Your throne, God, shall last for ever and ever,
   you royal sceptre is a sceptre of integrity:
   virtue you love as much as you hate wickedness.

   Psalm 45:6-7
   Hail Mary.

2.   This is why God, your God, has anointed you
   with the oil of gladness, above all your rivals;
   myrrh and aloes waft from your robes.   *Psalm 45:7-8*
   Hail Mary.

3.   From palaces of ivory harps entertain you,
   daughters of kings are among your maids of honour,
   on your right stands the queen, in gold from Ophir.

   Psalm 45:8-9
   Hail Mary.

4.   I came forth from the mouth of the Most High,
   and I covered the earth like a mist.
   I had my tents in the heights,
   and my throne in a pillar of cloud.

   Ecclesiasticus 24:5-7
   Hail Mary.

5.   Alone I encircled the vault of the sky,
   and I walked on the bottom of the deeps.

Over the waves of the sea and over the whole earth,
and over every people and nation I have held sway.

Ecclesiasticus 24:8-9
Hail Mary.

6. From eternity, in the beginning, he created me,
   and for eternity I shall remain.
   I ministered before him in the holy tabernacle,
   and thus was I established on Zion.
   In the beloved city he has given me rest,
   and in Jerusalem I wield my authority.

   Ecclesiasticus 24:14-15
   Hail Mary.

7. Approach me, you who desire me,
   and take your fill of my fruits,
   for memories of me are sweeter than honey,
   inheriting me is sweeter than the honeycomb.

   Ecclesiasticus 24:26-27
   Hail Mary.

8. They who eat me will hunger for more,
   they who drink me will thirst for more.
   Whoever listens to me will never have to blush,.
   whoever acts as I dictate will never sin.

   Ecclesiasticus 24:28-30
   Hail Mary.

9. The King has brought me into his rooms;
   you will be our joy and our gladness.

We shall praise your love above wine;
how right it is to love you.   *Song of Songs 1:4*

Hail Mary.

10. Let us be confident, then, in approaching the throne of
grace, that we shall have mercy from him and find
grace when we are in need of help.   *Hebrews 4:16*

Hail Mary.

Glory be to the Father.

Prayer

O God, your only begotten Son gained eternal life for us by his life, death and resurrection. May we who meditate on these mysteries in the holy rosary of the blessed Virgin Mary both follow the example that they give and obtain the salvation that they promise: through our Lord Jesus Christ your Son, who live and reigns with you in the unity of the Holy Spirit, one God, for ever and ever. Amen.